ALL ABOARD AMERICA

Lincoln Memorial

ABDO
Publishing Company

A Buddy Book
by
Julie Murray

VISIT US AT
www.abdopub.com

Published by Buddy Books, an imprint of ABDO Publishing Company, 4940 Viking Drive, Edina, Minnesota 55435. Copyright © 2003 by Abdo Consulting Group, Inc. International copyrights reserved in all countries. No part of this book may be reproduced in any form without written permission from the publisher.

Printed in the United States.

Edited by: Christy DeVillier
Contributing Editors: Matt Ray, Michael P. Goecke
Graphic Design: Deborah Coldiron
Image Research: Deborah Coldiron
Photographs: Digital Stock, Eyewire Inc., Library of Congress, Photodisc, Photospin

Library of Congress Cataloging-in-Publication Data

Murray, Julie, 1969-
   Lincoln Memorial / Julie Murray.
      p. cm. — (All aboard America)
   Includes bibliographical references and index.
   Summary: Discusses the construction, history, and current status of the Washington, D.C. monument to Abraham Lincoln and the freedom, equality, and justice he personified.
   ISBN 1-57765-670-9
      1. Lincoln Memorial (Washington, D.C.)—Juvenile literature. 2. Lincoln, Abraham, 1809-1865—Monuments—Juvenile literature. 3. Washington (D.C.)—Buildings, structures, etc.—Juvenile literature. [1. Lincoln Memorial (Washington, D.C.) 2. National monuments.] I. Title.

F203.4.L73 M87 2002
975.3—dc21

                                                                                        2001055244

Table of Contents

Lincoln Memorial

The Lincoln Memorial is a national **monument**. It honors President Abraham Lincoln. Many people believe Lincoln was one of the best United States presidents.

The Lincoln Memorial is in Washington, D.C. It is on the east bank of the Potomac River. It faces the Washington Monument and the Capitol.

The Lincoln Memorial
(LING-kun muh-MOR-ree-ul)

Detour

Did You Know?

Abraham Lincoln had a nickname. People called him "Honest Abe."

Abraham Lincoln

Young Abraham Lincoln lived in this log cabin.

Abraham Lincoln was born on February 12, 1809. He grew up in a log cabin in Kentucky. As a boy, Lincoln worked on his father's farm. Later, he became a lawyer and a lawmaker.

President Abraham Lincoln

Abraham Lincoln became the 16th U.S. president on March 4, 1861. He worked hard to end the **Civil War**. Lincoln is famous for ending **slavery**, too.

John Wilkes Booth shot and killed President Lincoln on April 14, 1865. This was a very sad day for Americans.

John Wilkes Booth shot President Lincoln at Ford's Theatre in Washington, D.C.

The Idea

Abraham Lincoln worked hard for his country. Americans did not want to forget Lincoln and his hard work. So, lawmakers talked about building a **monument** to him. Monuments help people remember important people and events.

Lincoln Memorial

Washington Monument

The Lincoln Memorial reminds people of President Lincoln.

United States leaders agree to set aside money for the Lincoln Memorial.

In 1911, the U.S. government agreed on building the Lincoln Memorial. At this time, William Howard Taft was the president. President Taft set aside two million dollars for the **monument**.

Henry Bacon was the **architect** of the Lincoln Memorial. Bacon believed American **democracy** was important to Abraham Lincoln. So, he designed the memorial to look like a Greek temple. Greece is the birthplace of democracy.

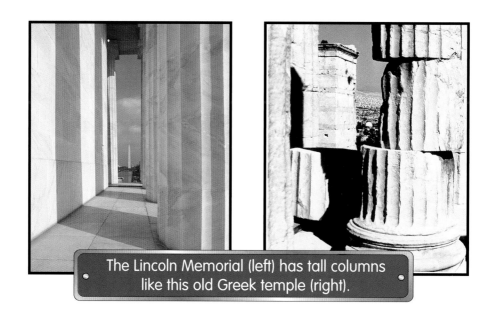

The Lincoln Memorial (left) has tall columns like this old Greek temple (right).

Some people call the Lincoln Memorial a "Temple of American Democracy."

The Lincoln Memorial has 36 columns. Each column is 44 feet (13 m) tall. The 36 columns stand for the 36 states governed by President Lincoln.

Two of Lincoln's greatest speeches are carved into the Lincoln Memorial's walls. These speeches are the Gettysburg Address and the Second Inaugural Address. Above each speech is a painting, or **mural**. Jules Guerin painted these murals. They honor President Lincoln's important accomplishments.

The Gettysburg Address is on one wall of the Lincoln Memorial.

The Lincoln Statue

The Lincoln statue is an important part of the Lincoln Memorial.

Daniel Chester French designed the Lincoln statue. Lincoln's closed fist stands for power. Lincoln's open right hand stands for his caring side.

Lincoln's Open Hand

Lincoln's Closed Fist

The Lincoln statue

The Piccirilli brothers from New York carved the Lincoln statue. They carved it from 28 white marble blocks.

Carving the great Lincoln statue.

It took eight years to build the Lincoln Memorial.

The Lincoln Memorial was finished in 1922. Over the years, many important events have happened there.

Dr. Martin Luther King, Jr.

In 1963, Dr. Martin Luther King, Jr. spoke at the Lincoln Memorial. This was Dr. King's famous "I Have a Dream" speech. Dr. King spoke about equal rights for African-Americans. Over 250,000 people were there for this important event.

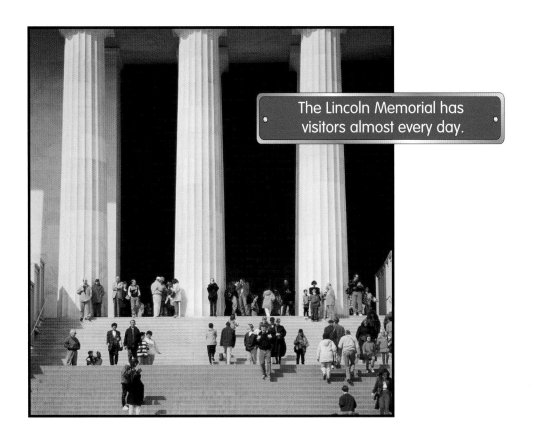

The Lincoln Memorial has visitors almost every day.

The Lincoln Memorial is open to visitors almost every day. It is closed on December 25th. Millions of people visit the Lincoln Memorial every year.

Important Words

architect (AR-kuh-tekt) a person who designs buildings, bridges, and other things.

Civil War (SIV-ul wor) the United States war between the Northern and the Southern states.

democracy (duh-MOCK-ruh-see) a nation that gives power to its people and believes in equal rights for all.

monument (MON-yoo-munt) something built to remind people of a special person or event.

mural (MYUR-ul) art painted on a wall.

slavery (SLAY-ver-ee) the act of owning people as slaves.

Web Sites

Would you like to learn more about the Lincoln Memorial?

Please visit ABDO Publishing Company on the information superhighway to find web site links about the Lincoln Memorial. These links are routinely monitored and updated to provide the most current information available.

www.abdopub.com

Index